Motion

Andrea Rivera

abdopublishing.com

Published by Abdo Zoom™, PO Box 398166, Minneapolis, Minnesota 55439. Copyright © 2018 by Abdo Consulting Group, Inc. International copyrights reserved in all countries. No part of this book may be reproduced in any form without written permission from the publisher. Abdo Zoom™ is a trademark and logo of Abdo Consulting Group, Inc.

Printed in the United States of America, North Mankato, Minnesota
052017
092017

THIS BOOK CONTAINS
RECYCLED MATERIALS

Cover Photo: iStockphoto
Interior Photos: iStockphoto, 1, 10, 11, 12–13, 16, 17, 21; Christopher Bernard/iStockphoto, 4; Fouad A. Saad/Shutterstock Images, 5; Rich Vintage/iStockphoto, 6; Shutterstock Images, 7, 8–9; Nor Gal/Shutterstock Images, 9; Supannee Hickman/Shutterstock Images, 15; Tomsickova Tatyana/Shutterstock Images, 19

Editor: Brienna Rossiter
Series Designer: Madeline Berger
Art Direction: Dorothy Toth

Publisher's Cataloging-in-Publication Data
Names: Rivera, Andrea, author.
Title: Motion / by Andrea Rivera.
Description: Minneapolis, MN : Abdo Zoom, 2018. | Series: Science concepts | Includes bibliographical references and index.
Identifiers: LCCN 2017931241 | ISBN 9781532120541 (lib. bdg.) | ISBN 978164797654 (ebook) | ISBN 978164798217 (Read-to-me ebook)
Subjects: LCSH: Motion--Juvenile literature.
Classification: DDC 531/.11--dc23
LC record available at http://lccn.loc.gov/2017931241

Table of Contents

Science

Motion is when an object changes position.

Objects move because of forces.
Forces can push an object.
They can also pull an object.

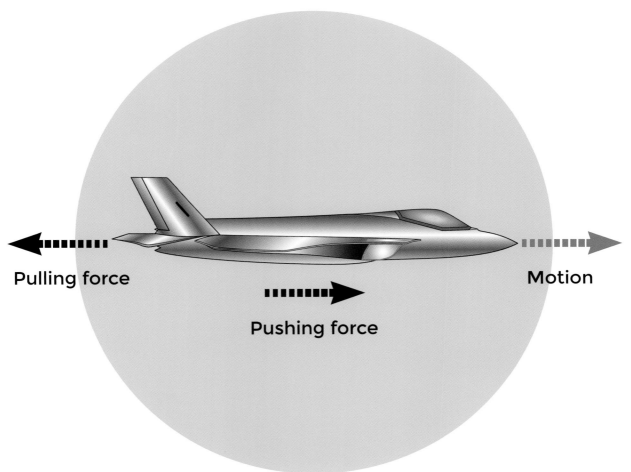

Pulling force

Pushing force

Motion

Forces make an object start moving. They make it stop moving, too.

They can also change the
direction it goes. A change in
motion is called acceleration.

Technology

Acceleration can mean speeding up. It can mean slowing down. Pedals control a car's acceleration.

The gas pedal makes the
car go faster. The brake
pedal makes it slow down.

Engineering

Falling is a kind of motion. Skydivers jump out of airplanes.

They fall toward the ground. **Gravity** pulls them down. It makes them fall faster and faster.

Parachutes make a force that pushes up. This slows the skydiver's fall.

Art

Kinetic sculptures use motion. They have parts that can move. Sometimes wind or water pushes on the parts. Other sculptures let viewers move them.

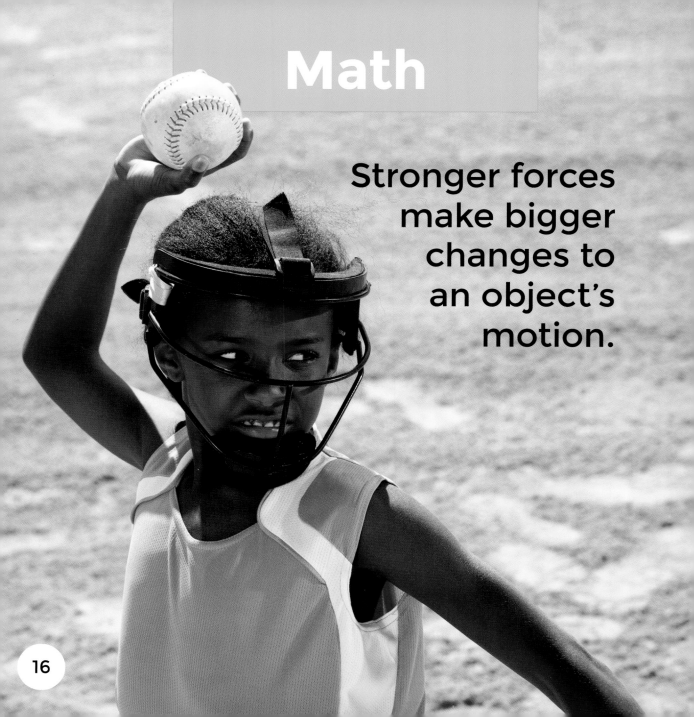

Math

Stronger forces make bigger changes to an object's motion.

Force is measured in **newtons**. A force of 30 newtons can move a bowling ball.

A force of 60 newtons is twice as strong. It will make the ball go twice as fast.

- In 1687 Isaac Newton used math to create three laws of motion. Scientists still use the laws today.

- Equal forces pushing from opposite directions cancel each other out. The object will not move.

- Moving objects will keep moving until a force stops them.

- Sometimes two objects bump into each other. The objects push each other. This can cause a change in motion.

Glossary

acceleration - a change in an object's speed or direction.

force - a push or pull that causes a change in motion.

gravity - a force that pulls things toward the center of the earth.

kinetic - related to movement.

newton - the unit used to measure force.

sculpture - an art form (such as a statue) that is three-dimensional, not flat.

Booklinks

For more information on
motion, please visit
abdobooklinks.com

 In on STEAM!

Learn even more with the Abdo Zoom
STEAM database. Check out
abdozoom.com for more information.

Index